Recharge

A Self-Awareness Approach to Goal Achievement

Dr. Kellie M Dixon, CPC

Recharge: A Self-Awareness Approach to Goal Achievement
Copyright © 2020 by Kellie M. Dixon

Printed in the United States of America
First Printing, 2020

ISBN 978-0-578-67391-2 (paperback)

Cover by: Jason Jeffress (Instagram: @jaibludesigns)

Dedication

This book is dedicated to the following:

my family/friends/loved ones/Kofi
my mentees
my colleagues in Higher Education
my supporters near and far
and YOU, the reader!

Table of Contents

Foreword 4

Introduction 6

Self-Awareness 7

Goals: Own, Rent, Lease 9

Holistic Wellness 10

Goals and Holistic Tasks 17

21-Day Recharge Plan 19

Resources 48

Foreword

It was truly an honor to have the pleasure of exhibiting the evolution of this book *RECHARGE*. I am confident this guide will assist individuals all over the world in the many phases of growth with aligning their lives to purpose on purpose through Dr. Dixon's unique approaches. This book will be used to manufacture, inspire and heal humans with an outcome to fully optimize an individual full potential and their calling as productive, healed humans in an ever changing global society.

For the past few years, I have personally benefited from lessons of Dr. Kellie Dixon. She is bright, articulate, and is truly a gem in the space of life coaching, consulting and unmasking hidden potential in budding professionals. This book is ideal for college students and young professionals as it serves as a conduit to managing everyday life, recovering from the unexpected and promoting inner potential through goal setting and personal accountability. *RECHARGE* takes readers on an adventure of self-reflection and goal setting that provides exercises to rethink norms and challenge critical thinking that will lead to discovery while documenting your journey.

Disruptions and unknown pathways are customary in life is inevitable; self-awareness requires self-examination. Be aware, though, that an honest, non-judgmental self-analysis isn't easy. We tend to berate ourselves for our failings or fantasize about how great we are, when neither is actually the case. Sometimes you don't need a mind changing philosophy, you just need the book *RECHARGE*. For every problem you have, *RECHARGE* challenges you to get to a solution with proven strategies that work.

I am excited about your decision to do the work required to be all you've been called to be. I am confident that *RECHARGE* is just the solution you've been mission. I wish you all a riveting and adventurous journey of discovery that will provide you the answers that will bring clarity to both your personal and professional lives.

God speed,
Dr. DeQuan M. Smith
Professor | Author | Consultant

4

Introduction

I began mentoring college students as early as 2009, which was during my first year of graduate school. My passion or helping others started long before college. However, it was during college that my passion became my purpose for life. When I began my career in higher education (specifically student affairs) in 2011, I began mentoring working professionals. Fast forward, due to the request of a few student mentees, I became a certified life coach in the summer of 2016. I pride myself in holistic and intentional mentorship, regardless of whether the individual is a student or a working professional. As a life coach, my philosophy is simple: *Align your why, how, and what; then remain consistent in your efforts*. As a mentor, it's even simpler: *When you are ready, I am here waiting on you.*

This book is about my experience and approach to achieving both personal and professional life goals. There is no right or wrong way toward goal achievement; however, I hope that this book will serve as a best practice for others as it has for my mentees, coaches, and myself. With a guiding framework, individuals can explore themselves in a more direct and intentional way that demonstrates self-awareness. Through self-awareness, we are able to strategically define our goals with holistic actions that contribute to our overall well-being.

I created the Recharge Experience to motivate individuals to look within for positive energy. You have enough positive energy within you to recharge daily and with the added support of accountability partners, you, too, can achieve every goal you define for yourself. The goal of this book is to serve as a resource and framework for understanding self-awareness and its link to goal achievement. The book is divided into different parts: (1) Self-Awareness; (2) Goals: Own, Rent, or Lease; (3) Holistic Wellness; (4) Goals and Tasks and the (5) 21-Day Recharge Plan. As you move through this book, I hope that you see the added value for yourself. and I welcome you to the Recharger Community!

With Much Appreciation,
Dr. Kellie M. Dixon "Dr. K"

Part 1: Self-Awareness

What does it mean to be self-aware? Well, let's break it down. *Self* refers to person's state of being, which makes that person unique compared to others. *Awareness* refers to perception of a something, place, or thing. Therefore, to be ***self-aware*** means the person has a perception of self that is unique to his or her existence.

Practicing Self

Practicing Self is my approach to understanding who I am and embracing my purpose in life. Most people feel as though they know who they are or are aware of themselves. I believe this is not far from the truth, but it is not all facts! We develop each day because of the decisions we make and the situations we encounter. It's life, and it's okay. I view Self-Awareness as the acceptance of who I am, who I want to be, and how others perceive me. Within Self-Awareness, there is Practicing Self, which consists of Self-forgiveness, Self-love, Self-reward, and Self-worth. Let me break down my philosophy!

Self-forgiveness

You have the right to be kind to yourself. You have your bad and good days; however, you cannot beat yourself up about it. Forgiving others is hard. Forgiving yourself is harder. We are our own worst critics. I am sure you have heard that line before. It is without a doubt true. We are human, and we must give ourselves permission to be just that: an imperfect human. When we forgive ourselves, we develop compassion for ourselves and that is the secret ingredient for a more meaningful life.

Self-love

At some point in your life, you have to protect yourself. You must come first! Self-love can be difficult. When you choose you, others may see it as being selfish. Well, don't mind that. It just means you need to be intentional about the boundaries you set with people. Loving yourself enables you to be mindful of your wants and needs. When you learn to love yourself, flaws and all, it will attract the right people in your life. The right people will honor your self-love. Your self-love will come with self-confidence, and it sure looks good on you!

Self-reward

There is nothing like accomplishing something and treating yourself for the hard work and commitment you put into doing that. You do not have to wait on others to celebrate you. Learn to celebrate your own self! You know what you like. Treat yourself because you deserve it. Remember this hard truth: many people will celebrate you in public and curse you in private.

Self-worth

It all comes down to this: knowing your worth! As stated before, you deserve the best there is in life; however, you have to believe that for yourself. You have to acknowledge your existence in this world and why you are of priceless value. You belong simply because there is only one you. The potential within you is worthy of respect from others and most importantly, YOU!

Part 2: Goals - Owning, Renting, or Leasing

I remember when I was asked the question: Are you owning, renting, or leasing? The context was in regards to my career; however, this question stuck with me, and I have found a way to apply it to goal setting and achievement. Let's explore the meaning behind these three terms for better understanding.

Leasing. The term *lease* is often used when purchasing a car. When you are leasing, simply put, you are agreeing to terms of something owned by someone else. You agree to a regular payment of some sort over an identified number of days, months, or years. In reference to your goals, I define leasing as *the act of agreeing to goals others have persuaded you to complete in order to achieve a certain milestone*. In other words, this is what I did to get here, and it took me two years; so, therefore, this is the roadmap you should follow to do the same.

Renting. The term *rent* is often using when obtaining an apartment or house. Typically, renting refers to a month-by-month contract in comparison to a lease. In reference to your goals, I define renting as the *act of choosing goals based on your current situation and circle of influence (or the company you keep)*. These goals shift monthly or very often without a solid foundation.

Owning. The term *own* refers to possessing something of your own where you make all decisions and agreements. You are responsible for all replacements and upkeep of that which you own. In reference to your goals, I define owning as *the act of applying Self-Awareness towards your own journey to success*. These goals are based on your understanding of your Self, your circle of influence, your capabilities, and your own declaration of success. You are the captain! Your choices and decisions dictate how and when you set and achieve goals. It is a combination of renting and leasing; however, the end result is your ownership of goals. Owning your goals will always have a consistent return of investment!

Part 3: Holistic Wellness

Holistic Wellness is an integrative approach that focuses on your mind, body, and soul consistently toward overall well-being. In 2018, I developed the Self Awareness Goal Setting Model which uses the concept of the Wellness Wheel and self-awareness to articulate an intentional way to create and achieve goals holistically. You can learn more about the model via www.clearpathwaycs.com. After reading this part of the books, use the Holistic Wellness Check (pg. 52) to see how aware you are in regards to your wellness. I use this to measure my holistic well-being and its alignment to my goals.

Emotional Wellness

Emotional wellness is awareness of one's own feelings. Your feelings are unique to you, and personal acceptance of them is critical to how you approach life. In today's society, it can be difficult showing your true emotions without feeling judged. Additionally, at times, we may find our feelings being denied by others. Therefore, societal input on our lives can have us demonstrating false emotions, while our true feelings are bottled up. Well, with bottled up emotions, you can go from zero to hundred really quick!

Our emotions can be one of the most horrific internal battles in our lives. Surpassing your own feelings is exhausting and for some people will get the best of you. The key word is "motion," and our emotions help us decide how and where we move. On any given day, our emotions can shift or even spiral out of control. Keep in mind, we all respond to situations differently with our emotions. Do not allow how others react impact your reaction. Your emotions matter, and, until you learn this, others will disregard them every time. Our emotional wellness has a way of impacting other dimensions of wellness.

Masking emotions

"Fake it until you make it!" This is a saying that many of us use so often. I used it, believing that it would push me to finish a task or get through a tough situation. I can report that it only made the experiences more draining. So, why even put myself in such a predicament? It may appear like an easy solution; however, masking emotions is difficult and negatively impacts all areas of life if you aren't careful. I have learned to understand my emotions and dig deeper for their true meaning. This concept allows me to effectively communicate how I truly feel and take the mask off. You owe it to yourself to be honest with emotions. The best relationship is the one you have with yourself. You may be able to lie to others, but you can't live happily telling lies to yourself. You deserve better and you can have better!

In relationships

Relationships, whether they are with friends, family, co-workers, or romantic interests, are the foundations for understanding and expressing different types of emotions. As humans, we are naturally concerned about how we make others feel and how they make us feel. Communication is key to emotional wellbeing in relationships of any kind. I recommend learning more about emotional intelligence. To ensure that our relationships are emotionally well, we can:

- Communicate feelings honestly without shame
- Have empathy with others
- Listen actively
- Accept feedback and/or criticism

Environmental Wellness

Environmental wellness is awareness and respect of our surroundings. The understanding of natural resources is key to environmental well-being. Understanding the world around us and the interaction we have with it may lead to harmonious living. Sometimes we do not appreciate the relationship of people and nature. When we learn to respect our environment, we live a lifestyle that keeps us from environmental hazards. These hazards include, but are not limited to chemicals, second-hand smoke, air pollution, and noise. When you see a problem in the environment, find ways to contribute to the solution!

Our environment can trigger various thoughts, both positive and negative. There is the saying, "You are a product of your environment." There is some truth to this statement, and it has an impact on our overall health. The choices we make in regards to our surroundings can lead to making better decisions in life. You have the opportunity to create the environment you want to live in. Every small step you take contributes to improvements in your environment.

The *waste hierarchy* consists of the 3 R's which include: reduce, reuse, recycle. **Reduce.** There are several methods to reduce waste, such as identify different ways to utilize items that are multipurpose. Various items that we purchase on a regular can be used for different purposes, if we just take the time to realize this simple observation. When you go to the grocery story, are you using reusable bags? When you have leftover foods, are you using washable and reusable food storage containers? Not only would you aide in reducing the amount of waste produced, yet save money in the process!

Reuse. It can be convenient and easy to throw away items that no longer serve a purpose to you. WAIT! Before you throw it away, think about how you can reuse that old, too big shirt (because you lost the weight you wanted) into a blanket. Additional, let's not forget about donating items or even selling them at a discounted price online (which is quite popular these days).

Recycle. This can be a tedious effort because not all recycle bins are created equal. Some differentiate between trash and paper/plastic. Others are more in depth of the separation of paper and plastic, among other items. Regardless of the recycle bin directions, take the extra time to recycle properly so that you can be a contributor to decreasing pollution!

The 3 R's help in conserving energy, landfills, and natural resources. Learn more about reducing, reusing, and recycling at www.epa.gov/recycle.

Financial Wellness

Financial wellness is awareness of your finances and learning ways to manage expenses. I would argue that financial concern is one of the top five reason of why we stay stressed. We can have too little money and constantly think about how we are going to make ends meet and provide the basic needs for ourselves and our families. On the flip side, we are financially stable, and everyone is looking to get into our pockets or we do not know how to manage finances, which can lead to bad financial decisions. Where is the happy medium here? Writing around financial wellness is stressing me out!

Regardless of how and when you talk about money, it impacts every aspect of your life. Discussing money is one of the most difficult conversations amongst couples, friends, or anyone for that matter. Too little money, there are problems! Then there is the concept of "more money, more problems". Regardless, it is a conversation that must be open and honest. Get a financial planner or talk with someone who continues to be a good steward of their money! I am not a financial planner nor a guru of the topic; however, I know that financial wellness is critical for achieving goals, whether directly or indirectly.

Individuals who practice financial literacy make decisions that impact both their present and future life on a daily basis. I recommend learning more about the different components of becoming financially literate. Financial literacy includes, but is not limited to, the following:

Budgeting
Credit
Investments
Life Insurance
Needs vs Wants
Retirement
Savings

Intellectual Wellness

Intellectual wellness is awareness and active participation in activities that involve educational advancement, cultural competency, and community involvement. Every day is an opportunity to learn something new and exciting that can lead toward living a happy and successful life. As you engage more intentionally about your intellect, creativity begins to surface. Creativity can serve as the foundation for living out dreams and being an active citizen in your community.

Occupational Wellness

Occupational wellness is awareness of oneself in the workplace and defining a professional identity. You have to figure out what occupations and tasks you enjoy doing and include even those that are less enjoyable. At any given time, we all experience stress in the workplace as we juggle work and life activities. Additionally, stress at work may lead to new career choices. A career or job can easily take up 30 or more hours of your time in a week. Therefore, it is important to understand your occupational needs and the impact of workplace stress on your life. Always find new ways to explore opportunities to enhance yourself in the workplace and professionally.

Physical Wellness

Physical wellness is the act of caring for your body for optimal function and health. There are many areas within physical wellness: exercise/physical activity, mental health, and nutrition. Our overall health benefits from being physically active by reducing risks of heart issues, strokes, and more. Additionally, an active lifestyle provides us more energy throughout the day. A few physical activity suggestions include: walking, yoga, hiking, weight lifting, and dance. It's recommended that you participate in 30 to 45 minutes of physical activity a day.

A balanced-diet is important to your physical wellness as well. There are many ways to ensure you receive the best nutrients on a daily basis to prevent and/or neutralize many health issues. Finally, mental well-being is a benefit from physical wellness. Mental health is also linked to other wellness areas, more specifically social and emotional wellness. Seeing a therapist is always a recommendation to assist in your mental well-being.

Mental health is the umbrella that covers every part of your wellness. Your mental health is a direct link to how you feel, act/behave, and think at any given moment. It is important that you keep your mental health at the forefront of your day. For example, I conduct daily mental health checks for myself and those around me through the use of a simple illustration. The illustration has been all over the internet and changed based on individual usage. Within the illustration, there are several different color hearts with phrases attached to them. For example, a yellow heart may mean "I'm doing okay, I guess". (If you search the internet, I am sure you will find exactly what I am referring to or if you visit my website at www.clearpathwaycs.com you can participate in an interactive version). This simple check-in will allow you to recognize where you are at any given moment so that you can be intentional about what you need from others and what you can give.

Social Wellness

Social wellness is all about the relationships and interactions we have with others. I am a firm believer that you must be aware of the company you keep. Know who you are connected to and who others are connected to as well. This is the idea of social capital, which contains the networks you maintain with various persons for a shared purpose or understanding. Social capital also involves how you and others provide resources for one another. This is very common in the workplace.

The concept of social wellness is not limited to family, colleagues, and friends. It also encompasses romantic relationships as well. Because we have different circles of networks and types of relationships, it is important to be able to balance and/or blend how they occupy space in our lives. You have to know your own social needs to ensure your wellness. And it is okay to let others know their purpose in your life and how you want them to show up. Establishing boundaries and having effective communication are key for maintaining social wellness.

Spiritual Wellness

Spiritual wellness allows us to find meaning and purpose for our lives. Spiritual wellness can be identified in various forms as it is not limited to our values, morals, religious affiliations, and ethical standards. Exploring your inner self is critical to your existence, overall wellness, and achieving goals. A common way of exploring your spiritual wellness is the practice of mindfulness. Mindfulness is the practice of being aware and focusing on oneself in the present moment. All in all, spiritual wellness is about finding what's important and letting it guide you!

Part 4: Defining Goals and Establishing Holistic Tasks

Alright, in working with individuals and even myself, I found that we are using goals and tasks interchangeably. These two words are not interchangeable and may be one of the reasons you aren't achieving goals effectively. Let's start by breaking down what each of these terms mean. A *goal* is a desired result within a defined timeframe. Whereas, a *task* is an action or assignment to be done. In my coaching, when I ask clients to provide me with their goals, they unconsciously began to name tasks. I must admit, I, too, would do the same before realizing that the tasks I named were attached to a deeper purpose or goal.

A task is simply an action you take to achieve your goals. Think of a goal as a means to an end! Therefore, there are many different tasks to help you reach a desired goal. This is where using the eight dimensions of wellness to define tasks is critical. I use these dimensions of wellness, because when we practice them all we, become more centered in who we are and what we desire in life. Once you define a goal, it will lead to the tasks you need to complete to achieve desired results. Also, I find it more fulfilling to use the holistic tasks approach to achieving a goal. This is because your tasks are directly aligned to your goal, and you become more intentional! Intentionality is key is goal achievement.

So, how do you identify the proper holistic actions? Great question! Here is my formula (no math experience needed)! Basically, for each goal, ask yourself the following question and answer it in every dimension of wellness: *What does it mean for me to [insert goal]?* Here is an example:

Goal: Travel to Africa.
1. What does it mean for me to take a trip to Africa emotionally? What emotions arise when I think about taking a trip to Africa that I need to address, if any? What tasks can I do to address this?
2. What does it mean for me to take a trip to Africa environmentally? What do I need to know about the environment that will be different than my present experiences? What tasks can I do to address this?

17

3. What does it mean for me to take a trip to Africa financially? What type of budget do I need, if any? What tasks can I do to address this?

4. What does it mean for me to take a trip to Africa occupationally? Do I have enough vacation time from work? If not, how can I acquire this time?

5. What does it mean for me to take a trip to Africa intellectually? What can I learn about Africa to prepare me, especially as it relates to tours, places to visit, etc.?

6. What does it mean for me to take a trip to Africa physically? Are there any physical limitations I may have? If so, how do I ensure that I address these prior to my visit?

7. What does it mean for me to take a trip to Africa socially? Am I going on this trip alone or with others? How will who I travel with impact my experience?

8. What does it mean for me to take a trip to Africa spiritually? Am I open to learning new beliefs as it relates to the culture of Africa?

Part 5: 21-Day Recharge Plan

Part 5 of this book provides a step-by-step plan to effectively participate in the 21-Day Recharge Experience. Additionally, after the steps are discussed, a copy of the "journal" is provided for your use. This experience is all about you and what you put into it. You probably will not get it "right," whatever that means, on the first try; however, let that be your motivation to keep doing it! I struggled myself a few times before I made it work for me and my goals. We are all human so we know good, bad, and ugly days will come; yet, it is how we challenge ourselves daily to be better versions of ourselves that make us who we are. So, I challenge you to fall and get back up again each day. I challenge you to take control of who you are and what you want and need out of life. I challenge you to make a positive difference in your life and the lives of others. I challenge you to be intentional about your own self-awareness and recharge daily to ensure you are the author of your story.

What is the 21-Day Recharge Plan?

I define "recharge" as the act of replenishing or restoring by connecting to another source of energy (preferably positive energy). In other words, often times we have the desire and initiative in us, we just need to be more proactive in recharging it. Understanding that every aspect of our being works together is the foundation for the 21-Day Recharge. This experience focuses on the eight (8) dimensions of holistic wellness: emotional, environmental, financial, intellectually, occupational, physical, social, and spiritual. Part 3 of this book discussed these dimensions in more detail as they relate to goal-setting. With the proper mindset and useful action plan, we can set and achieve goals more intentionally and strategically.

Why 21-Days?

Well, some say it takes 21 days to form or break habit. However, I feel there are no set days to do so. Nonetheless, I have found that working towards goals consistently with the proper support is both effective and efficient. Additionally, in working with mentees and coaches, I have found that 21 days are a great start toward changing your life to becoming more intentional about goal achievement.

My Commitment to YOU!

It is simple. Start now! There is no perfect time waiting on your around the corner to start working on your goals. If you are reading this workbook, then you have already completed the hard part: *you made the first step to show up for yourself.* You don't have to do this alone. Find an accountability partner. And remember, I am here to support you as well. Feel free to follow me on Twitter @clearpathway or send me an email at clearpathwaycs1@gmail.com. I am ready whenever you are!

Step 1: Schedule for Consistency

Create a schedule to follow for the next 21 days. The objective here is consistency (not necessarily the number of days). I have been able to achieve my goals simply because I was consistent in what I was doing on any given day towards my goals. This schedule is to be used for the next 21 days (Monday-Friday). Identifying what you do in a given day will help recognize where you currently spend your time and how you can find pockets of "flexible" time. The "flexible" time will be used towards intentional efforts for achieving your goals! Take a few moments to write out your current/typical day schedule based on Monday-Friday. Then use the template on page 49 to write out your 21-day schedule for recharging!

Step 2: Write Your Goals

Now that you have created your schedule for the next 21 days, you need to define your goals. These should be goals you can accomplish within the next 2 years. I don't call these short-term nor long-term goals, just goals to achieve within 2 years. As stated in Part 3, we must be intentional about what we want and realize that what we once defined as goals are simply results of accomplishing a more intentional goal. I won't say, "Come up with 10 or 5 goals." However, I will ask you to define four. Too many goals will overwhelm you, and you are less likely to accomplish them in a given timeframe. Remember, aspire to accomplish many goals, yet accomplish one goal at a time.

Step 3: Identify Your Holistic Actions

In Part 3, I discussed the eight dimensions of holistic wellness and their importance to goal setting and achievement. On page 51 of this book, you will find several examples of holistic actions you can use with goals (It's a simple list!). It is important that you take the time to think through your goals and the impact they have on your eight dimensions of wellness. This can be tough, however the previous section of this book breaks it down for better understanding. You won't get it right away, and that is okay. That's why I am here, tweet me (@clearpathway) or email me clearpathwaycs1@gmail.com if you get stuck and need some guidance. This step is the most important, in my opinion. This is the step where you begin to meld your self-awareness and goals together to create a life of holistic wellness. Will it be challenging? Of course; that's why you are doing it. Will it pay off? Absolutely; however, not without motivation, self-discipline, and the ability to choose You first!

Step 4: Journal Your Experiences

Writing out your goals and thoughts is not only therapeutic; it is also a commitment to who you are at that given moment. Individuals who write out goals and a plan of action are more likely to achieve their goals than those who do not write them out. This book provides you with a 21-day journal experience. You don't have to use the journal provided in the book (space is limited); however, you do need to journal. Therefore, it is okay if you use your own journal book. Maybe I will create a journal book to go with this book in the future!

In your writing, be honest and remember it's okay if you do not use complete sentences. These are your thoughts and your words. At the start, each you are asked to write out some affirmations. Affirmations keep us grounded when we need a "pick me up" or another voice of reason to keep pushing through. A list of my favorite affirmations can be found on page 53. Each day you are asked to provide your reflections and thoughts. On Sundays and Saturdays, you have questions to consider as you write out your thoughts. On the weekdays, in addition to your reflection and thoughts, you are asked to conduct a gratitude check and identify any self-rewards, if applicable. Examples of how to conduct a gratitude check is found on page 54.

Step 5: Reward Yourself
There is nothing like accomplishing something and treating yourself for the hard work and commitment you put in. You do not have to wait for others to celebrate you. Learn to celebrate your own self! You know what you like; treat yourself because you deserve it. Remember this hard truth: many people will celebrate you in public and curse you in private. Each day, consider how you can reward yourself. You can include these in your journal writing to keep track of your own self-care.

21 Day Recharge Plan

(The Journal)

Week 1

____ / ____ / ____ to ____ / ____ / ____

Write your affirmations here!

Sunday Reflection/Thoughts (Day 1)

_____

_____

_____

_____

_____

_____

_____

_____

_____

_____

_____

_____

_____

_____

_____

_____

_____

_____

_____

_____

_____

Questions to Consider

How are you feeling going into Week 1? What emotions are you having?

Monday Reflection/Thoughts (Day 2)

_____
_____
_____
_____
_____
_____
_____
_____
_____
_____
_____
_____
_____
_____
_____
_____
_____
_____
_____
_____
_____
_____

Gratitude Check/Reward Check (Day 2)

_____
_____
_____
_____

Tuesday Reflection/Thoughts (Day 3)

_____

_____

_____

_____

_____

_____

_____

_____

_____

_____

_____

_____

_____

_____

_____

_____

_____

_____

_____

_____

_____

_____

Gratitude Check/Reward Check (Day 3)

_____

_____

_____

_____

Wednesday Reflection/Thoughts (Day 4)

_____

_____

_____

_____

_____

_____

_____

_____

_____

_____

_____

_____

_____

_____

_____

_____

_____

_____

_____

_____

_____

_____

_____

Gratitude Check/Reward Check (Day 4)

_____

_____

_____

_____

Thursday Reflection/Thoughts (Day 5)

_____
_____
_____
_____
_____
_____
_____
_____
_____
_____
_____
_____
_____
_____
_____
_____
_____
_____
_____
_____
_____
_____
_____

Gratitude Check/Reward Check (Day 6)

_____
_____
_____
_____

Friday Reflection/Thoughts (Day 6)

_____

_____

_____

_____

_____

_____

_____

_____

_____

_____

_____

_____

_____

_____

_____

_____

_____

_____

_____

_____

_____

_____

Gratitude Check/Reward Check (Day 6)

_____

_____

_____

_____

Saturday Reflection/Thoughts (Day 7)

_____

_____

_____

_____

_____

_____

_____

_____

_____

_____

_____

_____

_____

_____

_____

_____

_____

_____

_____

_____

_____

_____

Questions to Consider

Are there any changes needed for Week 2 as they relate to your schedule? Goals? Holistic actions?

Week 2

____ / ____ / ____ to ____ / ____ / ____

Write your affirmations here!

Sunday Reflection/Thoughts (Day 8)

_____

_____

_____

_____

_____

_____

_____

_____

_____

_____

_____

_____

_____

_____

_____

_____

_____

_____

_____

_____

_____

_____

Questions to Consider

How are you feeling going into Week 2? What emotions are you having?

Monday Reflection/Thoughts (Day 9)

_____

_____

_____

_____

_____

_____

_____

_____

_____

_____

_____

_____

_____

_____

_____

_____

_____

_____

_____

_____

_____

_____

Gratitude Check/Reward Check (Day 9)

_____

_____

_____

_____

Tuesday Reflection/Thoughts (Day 10)

_____

_____

_____

_____

_____

_____

_____

_____

_____

_____

_____

_____

_____

_____

_____

_____

_____

_____

_____

_____

_____

Gratitude Check/Reward Check (Day 10)

_____

_____

_____

_____

Wednesday Reflection/Thoughts (Day 11)

_____

_____

_____

_____

_____

_____

_____

_____

_____

_____

_____

_____

_____

_____

_____

_____

_____

_____

_____

_____

_____

_____

Gratitude Check/Reward Check (Day 11)

_____

_____

_____

_____

Thursday Reflection/Thoughts (Day 12)

_____

_____

_____

_____

_____

_____

_____

_____

_____

_____

_____

_____

_____

_____

_____

_____

_____

_____

_____

_____

_____

_____

Gratitude Check/Reward Check (Day 12)

_____

_____

_____

_____

Friday Reflection/Thoughts (Day 13)

_____

_____

_____

_____

_____

_____

_____

_____

_____

_____

_____

_____

_____

_____

_____

_____

_____

_____

_____

_____

_____

_____

Gratitude Check/Reward Check (Day 13)

_____

_____

_____

_____

Saturday Reflection/Thoughts (Day 14)

_____

_____

_____

_____

_____

_____

_____

_____

_____

_____

_____

_____

_____

_____

_____

_____

_____

_____

_____

_____

_____

_____

Questions to Consider

Are there any changes needed for Week 3 as they relate to your
schedule? Goals? Holistic actions?

Week 3

_____ / _____ / _____ to _____ / _____ / _____

Write your affirmations here!

Sunday Reflection/Thoughts (Day 15)

_____
_____
_____
_____
_____
_____
_____
_____
_____
_____
_____
_____
_____
_____
_____
_____
_____
_____
_____
_____
_____
_____

Questions to Consider

How are you feeling going into Week 3? What emotions are you having?

Monday Reflection/Thoughts (Day 16)

_____

_____

_____

_____

_____

_____

_____

_____

_____

_____

_____

_____

_____

_____

_____

_____

_____

_____

_____

_____

_____

_____

_____

Gratitude Check/Reward Check (Day 16)

_____

_____

_____

_____

Tuesday Reflection/Thoughts (Day 17)

_____

_____

_____

_____

_____

_____

_____

_____

_____

_____

_____

_____

_____

_____

_____

_____

_____

_____

_____

_____

_____

_____

_____

Gratitude Check/Reward Check (Day 17)

_____

_____

_____

_____

Wednesday Reflection/Thoughts (Day 18)

_____

_____

_____

_____

_____

_____

_____

_____

_____

_____

_____

_____

_____

_____

_____

_____

_____

_____

_____

_____

_____

_____

_____

Gratitude Check/Reward Check (Day 18)

_____

_____

_____

_____

Thursday Reflection/Thoughts (Day 19)

_____
_____
_____
_____
_____
_____
_____
_____
_____
_____
_____
_____
_____
_____
_____
_____
_____
_____
_____
_____
_____
_____

Gratitude Check/Reward Check (Day 19)

_____
_____
_____
_____

Friday Reflection/Thoughts (Day 20)

_____

_____

_____

_____

_____

_____

_____

_____

_____

_____

_____

_____

_____

_____

_____

_____

_____

_____

_____

_____

_____

_____

Gratitude Check/Reward Check (Day 20)

_____

_____

_____

Saturday Reflection/Thoughts (Day 21)

_____
_____
_____
_____
_____
_____
_____
_____
_____
_____
_____
_____
_____
_____
_____
_____
_____
_____
_____
_____
_____
_____
_____

Questions to Consider

How was the last 21 days? Any you developing any new habits?
What further assistance do you need to achieve your goals? Have
you considered a Life Coach?

Resources

This section provides worksheets and resources that I use with clients and mentees toward goal achievement. Below is a list of resources included in this chapter:

The 21-Day Schedule (p. 49)
Goal Worksheet (p. 50)
Examples of Holistic Actions (p. 51)
Holistic Wellness Check (p. 52)
List of Affirmations (p. 54)
Gratitude Check (p. 55)

Copies of some resources can be downloaded at www.clearpathwaycs.com or by emailing me at clearpathwaycs1@gmail.com.

The 21 Day Schedule

TIME	ACTIVITY

EXAMPLE

TIME	ACTIVITY
5:00AM – 5:30AM	MEDITATION/MINDFULNESS READING
5:45AM – 6:30AM	GYM
6:45AM – 7:15 AM	SHOWER/GET DRESSED
7:15AM -7:45AM	EAT BREAKFAST
8:00AM – 5:00PM	WORK (W/1 HOUR LUNCH 12PM-1PM)
5:15PM-6:00PM	SHOWER/UNWIND FROM WORK
6:00PM-7:00PM	COOK AND EAT DINNER
7:00PM-10:00PM	FLEX TIME/WORK ON GOAL (S)
10:00PM	GO TO BED

Goal Worksheet

RECHARGE YOUR GOAL WORKSHEET

MY GOAL:

SUPPORT NEEDED:

CHALLENGES:

HOLISTIC ACTIONS		MY REWARDS INCLUDE
	DONE!	
Emotional	_____	
Environmental	_____	
Financial	_____	
Intellectual	_____	NOTES
Occupational	_____	
Physical	_____	
Social	_____	
Spiritual	_____	

Examples of Holistic Actions

Emotional: participate in one random act of kindness a week

Environmental: eat at one local restaurant a week; recycle daily; reduce amount of paper used

Financial: create a monthly budget; save 10% of paycheck a month

Intellectual: read one book a month; participate in a book club; listen to a podcast

Occupational: complete one professional development activity a month; take a career appraisal assessment

Physical: commit to 30 minutes of walking each day; create a monthly diet plan

Social: choose 2 days a month to spend time with friends

Spiritual: meditate for 15 minutes each morning after waking up

Holistic Wellness Check

EMOTIONAL AWARENESS CHECK

	NEVER	SOMETIMES	OFTEN
I communicate my emotions.			
I get frustrated easily.			
It is hard to move on when unhappy.			
I recognize my own emotions.			

ENVIRONMENTAL AWARENESS CHECK

	NEVER	SOMETIMES	OFTEN
I recycle.			
I am aware of my surroundings.			
I buy locally grown foods.			
I use reusable shopping bags.			

FINANCIAL AWARENESS CHECK

	NEVER	SOMETIMES	OFTEN
I use a monthly budget.			
I live within my means.			
I assess my finances.			
I communicate about finances.			

INTELLECTUAL AWARENESS CHECK

	NEVER	SOMETIMES	OFTEN
I find new ways to be creative.			
I appreciate differences in people.			
I explore the world I live in.			
I seek ways to develop intellectually.			

OCCUPATIONAL AWARENESS CHECK

	NEVER	SOMETIMES	OFTEN
I enjoy going to work.			
I have a work/life balance.			
I communicate effectively with co-workers.			
I explore different career choices.			

PHYSICAL AWARENESS CHECK

	NEVER	SOMETIMES	OFTEN
I exercise.			
I get an adequate of sleep.			
I get physical exams.			
I eat a well-balanced meals daily.			

SOCIAL AWARENESS CHECK

	NEVER	SOMETIMES	OFTEN
I make time for people.			
I value diverse perspectives.			
I understand how I show up in different social settings.			
I empathize with people.			

SPIRITUAL AWARENESS CHECK

	NEVER	SOMETIMES	OFTEN
I explore my own being.			
I examine my beliefs.			
I explore new beliefs.			
I meditate.			

NEVER – Review ways to enhance your awareness.
SOMETIMES – Good job, it's all about consistency.
OFTEN – Great awareness!

Affirmations

(Some of Dr. K's affirmations!)

I acknowledge the work I need to do and do it.

I am worth my own investment.

Everyone has a perception of me; however, only I know my purpose.

I know my strengths and I know when I need help.

Other people's expectations of me are not aligned with my experiences. I will live my own life.

God didn't create two people alike, so why should I compare myself to others. My time will come.

I will give myself loving kindness daily, even when it's difficult.

Execute. Elevate. Then BossUp!

Gratitude Check

Statement	I am consistent	I can do better	I am not doing this
I am thankful for what others have done for me			
I am thankful for my relationships			
I tell people I appreciate them			
I am thankful for my surroundings			
I am always thinking of ways to help people			
I say thank you			
I don't take my possessions for granted			
I don't take people in my life for granted			
I am thankful for my existence			

Notes/References

Notes/References

About the Author
Dr. Kellie M. Dixon, CPC

"And let us not be weary in well doing: for in due season we shall reap, if we faint not." Galatians 6:9 (KJV)

Dr. Kellie M. Dixon received an Associate of Science degree in Science from Danville Community College, a Bachelor of Science degree in Kinesiology and Master of Science degree in Community and College Counseling from Longwood University. In addition, she received a doctorate from Grand Canyon University in Organizational Leadership with an emphasis in Organizational Development.

Dr. Dixon is a Certified Life Coach through the Life Coach Institute of Orange County. As a well-respected and sought after consultant, life coach, and mentor, Dr. Dixon is committed to the holistic well-being and achievement of both individuals and organizations. She is well-known for her commitment to the progression and experiences of both students and faculty/staff at HBCUs through her work in institutional effectiveness (i.e. accreditation and assessment) and staff development.

A Virginia, back roads, country native, Dr. Dixon is the founder of Clear Pathway Consulting Services, LLC, where she uses her passion for helping others through holistic wellness coaching, higher education consulting, and career coaching. Dr. Dixon is a well-respected colleague in higher education and is the 2020 recipient of the Outstanding Mentor to New Professionals Award, presented by the American College Personal Association's Graduate Students and New Professionals – Community of Practice. When she's not coaching, consulting, or mentoring, Dr. Dixon enjoys listening/dancing to music, traveling, and spending time with family, friends, loved ones, and her four-legged son, Kofi. She is a proud member of Zeta Phi Beta Sorority, Inc.

Made in the USA
Middletown, DE
15 October 2020